# Handy North Carolina Genealogy Handbook

## By Gary L. Morris

©2015 Gary L. Morris

ISBN-13: 978-1506173436

ISBN-10: 1506173438

# Table of Contents

# Notes

## Genealogical Research in North Carolina

As it is one of the oldest American states, there are many genealogical records and resources available for tracing your family history in North Carolina. Because there are so many records held at many different locations, tracking down the records for your ancestor can be an ominous task. Don't worry though, we know just where they are, and we'll show you which records you'll need, while helping you to understand:

1. What they are
2. Where to find them
3. How to use them

These records can be found both online and off, so we'll introduce you to online websites, indexes and databases, as well as brick-and-mortar repositories and other institutions that will help with your research in North Carolina. So that you will have a more comprehensive understanding of these records, we have provided a brief history of the "Old North State" to illustrate what type of records may have been generated during specific time periods. That information will assist you in pinpointing times and locations on which to focus the search for your North Carolina ancestors and their records.

## A Brief History of North Carolina

Living in North Carolina at the time the first Europeans arrived were the Native American tribes of the Siouan, Algonkian, and Iroquoian-language families. The Cherokees were the largest of the Iroquoian speaking tribes, although the Chowanoc, Hatteras, Meherrin, Roanoke, and other Algonkian speaking tribes had probably lived in the area the longest.

Giovanni da Verrazano, an Italian explorer working for the French government discovered the coast of North Carolina in 1524. The Spanish unsuccessfully attempted to establish a settlement at the mouth of the Cape Fear River in 1526, and Hernando de Soto explored the area for gold 1540, but to no avail. The Spanish influence on the area was minimal, but when the English arrived under the leadership of Sir Walter Raleigh sixty years later, the effect would be irreversible.

Explorers sent by Sir Walter Raleigh arrived on the Outer Banks in 1584 and sent back reports so encouraging that Raleigh decided to sponsor the founding of a colony on Roanoke Island. In three attempts over the next three years the English failed to establish a permanent settlement, but during that time the first child born of English parents in the New World, Virginia Dare, was born. Finally the English focused on a more realistic area, and the colony of Jamestown in Virginia was established. North Carolina would remain devoid of whites until 1653 when settlers arrived in Albemarle Sound from Virginia.

In 1663 Charles II granted the area to eight of his benefactors who divided Carolina as it was then called, into three counties, a separate governor appointed for each. Relations between the settlers who had come from Virginia and the new government that had been imposed on them were frayed, especially by attempts to heavily tax them. This antagonism led to one of the first acts of rebellion against the British in America, the Culpepper's Rebellion of 1677. The rebellion gained the settlers better representation in government, but things again went awry when the government attempted to reinforce the positions of the Anglican Church in the region. Laws were passed against the Quakers which sparked another uprising, Cary's Rebellion in 1711. The Tuscarora Indians saw an opportunity during the confusion and launched their rebellion against the white settlers; however they were defeated in 1713.

Political impotence in the north caused the southern part of the colony to split off in 1719, and ten years later when all of the original proprietors but one relinquished their rights to the area, North Carolina became a Royal Colony. Thousands of settlers flocked to the new colony, and by 1775 North Carolina had one of the largest populations in the New World, approximately 350,000. Germans and Scots-Irish arrived from Pennsylvania, while more Scottish and English settlers continued to come from Europe. Those who settled in the back country practiced self-sufficient farming, but the east coast settlers established tobacco and rice plantations which they staffed with slave labor.

North Carolina joined the battle for American independence in 1776, and though support for the British was manifested among Scottish immigrants, the colony remained loyal to the cause. Little action took place in North Carolina until the latter stages of the war, and North Carolina finally ratified the US Constitution in November of 1789. Prosperity was slow to come to the new state however, and it wasn't until social reforms in the state constitution in 1853 provided state aid to railroads and other public works.

As in other southern states, the white majority in North Carolina opposed emancipation, and ceded from the Union in 1861. More troops were provided for the Confederate cause from North Carolina than any other state, but support for the war was mixed. The state became a haven for deserters from the Richmond front due to opposition to the conscription policies of the Confederacy, and Union settlements flourished in the mountain areas. Most North Carolinians stood with the Confederate cause to the end however, which led to bitter political and social struggles during the Reconstruction Era.

Republican abolitionists fought for the rights of freedmen, while the slaveholding elite retaliated with intimidation and violence under the white robes and hoods of the Ku Klux Klan. Attempts by governor Holden to establish order were ineffective, and he was impeached in 1870 when Conservatives captured the General Assembly. The reconstruction Era came to an end in 1876 when a Conservative governor was elected, but racial troubles would continue well into the 20th century.

**Important Dates in North Carolina History**

**1653** – Settlers arrive at Albemarle Sound from Virginia

**1663** – Charles II grants area to eight of his benefactors

**1677** – Culpepper's Rebellion

**1711** – Cary's Rebellion and Tuscarora War

**1712** – North and South Carolina divided into separate provinces

**1729** – North Carolina becomes a Royal Colony

**1789** – Ratifies US Constitution

**1861** – Cedes from Union

**1868** – Readmitted to Union

**Famous Battles Fought in North Carolina**

There were quite a few skirmishes in North Carolina during the Revolutionary War, including a couple of major battles. A full listing of these battles and their accounts can be found at the **Revolutionary War Battlefields in North Carolina** webpage.

There were also quite a few battles fought in North Carolina during the Civil War, including two decisive engagements, one major conflict, and at least a dozen other principal engagements. You can read accounts of these battles at the **Battles in North Carolina** webpage.

These battle accounts that exist can be very effective in uncovering the military records of your ancestor. They can tell you what regiments fought in which battles, and often include the names and ranks of many officers and enlisted men.

**Revolutionary War Battlefields in North Carolina**:
http://ncrevwar.lostsoulsgenealogy.com/battlefieldsnc.htm

**Battles in North Carolina**:
http://nccivilwar.lostsoulsgenealogy.com/nccwbattle.htm

**Common North Carolina Genealogical Issues and Resources to Overcome Them**

**Boundary Changes**: Boundary changes are a common obstacle when researching North Carolina ancestors. You could be searching for an ancestor's record in one county when in fact it is stored in a different one due to historical county boundary changes.

The **Atlas of Historical County Boundaries** can help you to overcome that problem. It provides a chronological listing of every boundary change that has occurred in the history of North Carolina.

**Atlas of Historical County Boundaries** link to: http://publications.newberry.org/ahcbp/documents/NC_Consolidated_Chronology.htm#Consolidated_Chronology

**Name Changes**: Surname changes, variations, and misspellings can complicate genealogical research. It is important to check all spelling variations. Soundex, a program that indexes names by sound, is a useful first step, but you can't rely on it completely as some name variations result in different Soundex codes. The surnames could be different, but the first name may be different too. You can also find records filed under initials, middle names, and nicknames as well, so you will need to **get creative with surname variations** and spellings in order to cover all the possibilities. For help with surname variations read our instructional article on **How to Use Soundex**.

**get creative with surname variations**: http://obituarieshelp.org/blog/?p=634

**How to Use Soundex**: http://obituarieshelp.org/blog/?p=505

# North Carolina Genealogical Organizations and Archives

Genealogical resources include not only records, but the organizations that house them, or can direct you to them. These institutions include: *Archives, Libraries, Genealogical Societies, Family History Centers, Universities, Churches, and Museums.*

Following are links to their websites, their physical addresses, and a summary of the records you can find there.

<u>Archives and Libraries</u>

**State Archives of North Carolina** - census records, military records, manuscripts, newspapers, county records, state government records, historical photographs, maps, church and cemetery records, vital records, and more

State Archives of North Carolina
109 E. Jones St.
Raleigh, North Carolina 27601
Phone: (919) 733-3952

**State Archives of North Carolina**:
http://www.ncdcr.gov/archives/Public/Collections.aspx

**North Carolina State Library** - family histories, published abstracts, periodicals, military database, historical newspapers, wills, deeds, and census indexes

109 E. Jones St.
Raleigh, North Carolina 27601
Phone: 919-807-7460

**North Carolina State Library**:
http://statelibrary.ncdcr.gov/ghl/resources/genealogy.html

**National Archives Southeast Region (Atlanta)** – census records, non-population and mortality schedules from 1790-1920,

5780 Jonesboro Road
Morrow, Georgia 30260
Telephone: 770-968-2100
Fax: 770-968-2547
Email: atlanta.archives@nara.gov

**National Archives Southeast Region (Atlanta)**:
http://www.archives.gov/atlanta/finding-aids/index.html

North Carolina Genealogical and Historical Societies

Genealogical and historical societies have access to extensive catalogues of genealogical data. They are also able to offer expert guidance for genealogical researchers. Many members are professional genealogists who are most willing to share their expertise in finding ancestors.

**North Carolina Genealogical Society** – wide variety of genealogical resources for researching North Carolina ancestors

PO Box 22
Greenville, NC 27835-0022

**North Carolina Genealogical Society**:
http://www.ncgenealogy.org/

**Additional Resources**

North Carolina Mailing Lists

Mailing lists are internet based facilities that use email to distribute a single message to all who subscribe to it. When information on a particular surname, new records, or any other important genealogy information related to the mailing list topic becomes available, the subscribers are alerted to it. Joining a mailing list is an excellent way to stay up to date on North Carolina genealogy research topics. Rootsweb have an extensive listing of **North Carolina Mailing Lists** on a variety of topics.

**North Carolina Mailing Lists**:
http://lists.rootsweb.ancestry.com/index/usa/NC/misc.html

North Carolina Message Boards

A message board is another internet based facility where people can post questions about a specific genealogy topic and have it answered by other genealogists. If you have questions about a surname, record type, or research topic, you can post your question and other researchers and genealogists will help you with the answer. Be sure to check back regularly, as the answers are not emailed to you. The message boards at the **Rootsweb Website** are completely free to use.

**Rootsweb Website:**
http://boards.rootsweb.com/localities.northam.usa.states.northcarolina/mb.ashx

## North Carolina Newspapers and Periodicals

Many genealogy periodicals and historical newspapers contain reprinted copies of family genealogies, transcripts of family Bible records, information about local records and archives, census indexes, church records, queries, land records, obituaries, court records, cemetery records, and wills. The following sites have historical North Carolina newspapers and periodicals that you can search online or on-site.

**North Carolina State Library** – historical newspapers and periodicals dating from 1751

109 E. Jones St.
Raleigh, North Carolina 27601
Phone: 919-807-7460

**North Carolina State Library**:
http://statelibrary.ncdcr.gov/ghl/resources/genealogy.html

**GenealogyBank.com** – free searchable database of North Carolina newspaper archives, 1787-1993

**GenealogyBank.com**:
http://www.genealogybank.com/gbnk/newspapers/explore/USA/Nort h_Carolina/

**The Online Books Page** – links to historical North Carolina books and periodicals available for viewing online

**The Online Books Page**:
http://onlinebooks.library.upenn.edu/webbin/book/browse?type=subj ect&c=c&key=north+carolina

**Library of Congress Digital Newspaper Directory** – free searchable database of historical U.S. newspapers dating from 1690-present

**Library of Congress Digital Newspaper Directory**:
http://chroniclingamerica.loc.gov/search/titles/

Historical North Carolina Maps and Gazetteers

Maps are an integral part of genealogical research. They help us to
locate landmarks, towns, cities, parishes, states, provinces,
waterways and roads and streets. They also help us to determine
when and where boundary changes might have taken place, and give
us a visualization of the area we're researching in.

For locating place names, a gazetteer is the best possible resource for
any genealogist. Gazetteers are also sometimes called "place name
dictionaries", and can help you to locate the area in which you need
to conduct research. Below are links to the maps and gazetteers for
research in North Carolina.

**Peabody GNIS Service – North Carolina**:
http://peabody.research.yale.edu/cgi-
bin/Query.GNIS?ST=North%20Carolina&SU=1

**Color Landform Atlas – North Carolina**:
http://fermi.jhuapl.edu/states/nc_0.html

**1985 U.S. Atlas**: http://www.livgenmi.com/1895/NC/

**North Carolina Hometown Locator**:
http://northcarolina.hometownlocator.com/

## North Carolina City Directories

.

City directories are similar to telephone directories in that they list the residents of a particular area. The difference though is what is important to genealogists, and that is they pre-date telephone directories. You can find an ancestor's information such as their street address, place of employment, occupation, or the name of their spouse. A one-stop-shop for finding city directories in North Carolina is the **North Carolina Online Historical Directories** which contains a listing of every available online historical directory related to North Carolina.

**North Carolina Online Historical Directories**: https://sites.google.com/site/onlinedirectorysite/Home/usa/nc

Additionally the **North Carolina Digital Heritage Center** has an online database of almost one thousand directories from the years 1860 through 1963

**North Carolina Digital Heritage Center**: http://digitalnc.org/collections/north-carolina-city-directories

# North Carolina Genealogical Records

<u>Birth, Death, Marriage and Divorce Records</u> – Also known as vital records, birth, death, and marriage certificates are the most basic, yet most important records attached to your ancestor. The reason for their importance is that they not only place your ancestor in a specific place at a definite time, but potentially connect the individual to other relatives. Below is a list of repositories and websites where you can find North Carolina vital records.

**North Carolina Department of Health and Human Resources** – Birth Certificates, 1913-Present; Death Certificates, 1930-Present; Marriage Certificates, 1962-Present; Divorce Certificates, 1958-Present; Fetal Death Reports, 2001-Present

North Carolina Vital Records (Cooper Memorial Health Building)
225 N. McDowell St.
Raleigh, NC 27603-1382
Telephone: 919-733-3000
Fax: 919-733-1511

**Mailing Address**:

North Carolina Vital Records
1903 Mail Service Center
Raleigh, NC 27699-1903

**North Carolina Department of Health and Human Resources**
link to: http://vitalrecords.nc.gov/

**State Archives of North Carolina** – County birth, death, marriage, and divorce records dating from the 18th century

State Archives of North Carolina
109 E. Jones St.
Raleigh, North Carolina 27601
Phone: (919) 733-3952

**State Archives of North Carolina** link to:
http://www.ncdcr.gov/archives/Public/Collections.aspx

**Family Search** has the following indexes which can be searched online for free:

**North Carolina, Birth Index, 1800-2000**:
https://familysearch.org/search/collection/1949336

**North Carolina, Births and Christenings, 1866-1964**:
https://familysearch.org/search/collection/1675484

**North Carolina, County Marriages, 1762-1979**:
https://familysearch.org/search/collection/1726957

**North Carolina, Davidson County Vital Records, 1867-1984**:
https://familysearch.org/search/collection/1387049

**North Carolina, Deaths and Burials, 1898-1994**:
https://familysearch.org/search/collection/1675510

**North Carolina, Deaths, 1906-1930** :
https://familysearch.org/search/collection/1609799

**North Carolina, Deaths, 1931-1994** :
https://familysearch.org/search/collection/1584959

**North Carolina, Marriages, 1759-1979**:
https://familysearch.org/search/collection/1675514

Census Reports

**Census records** are among the most important genealogical documents for placing your ancestor in a particular place at a specific time. Like BDM records, they can also lead you to other ancestors, particularly those who were living under the authority of the head of household.

Federal census records for North Carolina exist from 1790–1930 and can be found at:

**State Archives of North Carolina** – census records, 1787-1920

State Archives of North Carolina
109 E. Jones St.
Raleigh, North Carolina 27601
Phone: (919) 733-3952

**State Archives of North Carolina**:
http://www.ncdcr.gov/archives/Public/Collections.aspx

**North Carolina State Library** - federal census population census schedules, 1800-1930, federal census slave schedules, 1850 and 1860, federal mortality schedules,1850-1880, federal agricultural, industrial, and social statistics schedules, 1850-1880

109 E. Jones St.
Raleigh, North Carolina 27601
Phone: 919-807-7460

**North Carolina State Library**:
http://statelibrary.ncdcr.gov/ghl/resources/genealogy.html

**National Archives** – Federal census Schedules for all states, 1790-1940

8601 Adelphi Road
College Park, MD 20740-6001
Tel: 1-866-272-6272

**National Archives** link to:
http://www.archives.gov/research/census/

The **Free Census Project** has transcribed many North Carolina indexes and new material is added daily

**Free Census Project** : http://usgwcensus.org/cenfiles/nc.htm

**Access Genealogy** – North Carolina county census records from 1790-1930

**Access Genealogy**: http://www.accessgenealogy.com/census/north-carolina-census-records.htm

**African American Census Schedules Online** – slave schedules, mortality schedules, slave-owners census

**African American Census Schedules Online**:
http://www.afrigeneas.com/aacensus/ga/

**Native Americans in Census Records** (US National Archives)

**Native Americans in Census Records**:
http://www.archives.gov/research/census/native-americans/

North Carolina Church Records

Church and synagogue records are a valuable resource, especially for baptisms, marriages, and burials that took place before 1900. You will need to at least have an idea of your ancestor's religious denomination, and in most cases you will have to visit a brick and mortar establishment to view them.

Most church records are kept by the individual church, although in some denominations, records are placed in a regional archive or maintained at the diocesan level. Local Historical Societies are sometimes the repository for the state's older church records. Below are links archives that maintain church records, as well as a few databases that can be viewed online.

The **Family History Library** contains many church records from a variety of denominations on microfilm.

**Family History Library**:
http://familysearch.org/learn/wiki/en/Family_History_Library

**Special Collections at Belk Library** - Miscellaneous Church Records, 1791 - 1991

Boone, NC 28608 USA
Phone: 828-262-404
Email: Via online contact form

**Special Collections at Belk Library** :
http://www.collections.library.appstate.edu/findingaids/ac218

## Central Repositories for Denominational Records

Church of Jesus Christ of Latter-day Saints (Mormons)

Early Mormon Church records for North Carolina can be found on film located at the LDS Family History Library in Salt Lake City and can be searched via the **Family History Library Catalog**

**Family History Library Catalog**:
https://familysearch.org/eng/Library/FHLC/frameset_fhlc.asp

Baptist

**Baptist Historical Collection**
Z. Smith Reynolds Library
Wake Forest University
P.O. Box 7777
Winston-Salem, NC 27109-7777
Telephone: 336-758-5089
Fax: 336-758-5605

**Baptist Historical Collection**:http://wakespace.lib.wfu.edu/handle/10339/33589

Presbyterian

**Presbyterian Historical Society**
United Presbyterian Church in the USA
425 Lombard Street
Philadelphia, Pennsylvania 19147
Telephone: (215) 627-1852

**Presbyterian Historical Society**: http://www.history.pcusa.org/

Church of England (Anglican, Episcopal)

**Diocese of North Carolina**
200 West Morgan Street
Suite 300
Raleigh, NC 27619
Telephone: 919-834-7474
or 1-800-448-8775
Fax: 919-834-7546

**Diocese of North Carolina**: http://www.episdionc.org/

**Diocese of Western North Carolina**
900-B Central Park Drive
Asheville, NC 28805
Telephone: 828-225-6656
Fax 828-225-6657
E-mail: bishop@diocesewnc.org

**Diocese of Western North Carolina**: http://www.diocesewnc.org/

**Diocese of East Carolina**
705 Doctors Drive
P. O. Box 1336
Kingston, NC 28503
Telephone: 252-522-0885
Fax 252-532-5272
E-mail: diocese@diocese-eastcarolina.org

**Diocese of East Carolina**: http://www.diocese-eastcarolina.org/

<u>Disciples of Christ</u>

**Discipliana Collections**
Barton College
Wilson, NC 27893
Telephone: 252-399-6352
Toll Free:  1-800-345-4973

**Discipliana Collections** : http://www.barton.edu/

<u>Lutheran</u>

**Archives, North Carolina Synod**
Lutheran Church in America
1988 Lutheran Synod Dr.
Salisbury, NC 28144-5700
Telephone: 704-633-4861
Fax: 704-638-0508

**Archives, North Carolina Synod**: http://www.nclutheran.org/

<u>Methodist</u>

**United Methodist Church Archives**
P.O. Box 127 Drew University
36 Madison Ave.
Madison, NJ 07940-3189
Telephone: 973-408-3189
Fax: 973-408-3909
E-mail: research@gcah.org

**United Methodist Church Archives** :
http://www.gcah.org/site/c.ghKJI0PHIoE/b.2858857/k.BF4D/Home.
htm

Moravian

**Moravian Archives**
457 South Church Street
Winston-Salem, NC 27101
Telephone: 336-722-1742
E-mail: moravianarchives@mcsp.org

**Moravian Archives** : http://moravianarchives.org/

Roman Catholic

**Archives of the Diocese of Raleigh**
The Catholic Center
715 Nazareth Street
Raleigh, NC 27603
Telephone: 919-821-9700
Fax: 919-821-9705

**Archives of the Diocese of Raleigh**:
http://www.dioceseofraleigh.org/home/index.aspx

**Archives of the Diocese of Charlotte**
1524 East Morehead St.
P.O. Box 36776
Charlotte, NC 28236
Telephone: 704-377-6871
Fax: 704-358-1208

**Archives of the Diocese of Charlotte**:
http://www.charlottediocese.org/

<u>Society of Friends (Quakers)</u>

**Friends Historical Collection**
Hege Library
5800 West Friendly Ave.
Greensboro, NC 27410-4175
Telephone: 336-316-2000
Fax: 336-316-2950
E-mail: mchijiok@guilford.edu

**Friends Historical Collection**: http://library.guilford.edu/

North Carolina Military Records

More than 40 million Americans have participated in some time of war service since America was colonized. The chance of finding your ancestor amongst those records is exceptionally high. Military records can even reveal individuals who never actually served, such as those who registered for the two World Wars but were never called to duty.

Below are a number of links to websites and archives that contain North Carolina military records.

**State Archives of North Carolina** – WWI and WWII records, Confederate records, Military pensions records, Court Martial minutes, Veterans rosters, Roll Books, Muster Rolls, Revolutionary War Loyalists Papers and more

State Archives of North Carolina
109 E. Jones St.
Raleigh, North Carolina 27601
Phone: (919) 733-3952

**State Archives of North Carolina**:
http://www.ncdcr.gov/archives/Public/Collections.aspx

**National Archives Southeast Region (Atlanta)** – Revolutionary war records, Civil war records, Indian wars records, Mexican War records, Veterans Pension records, Philippine Insurrection records, Spanish American War records

5780 Jonesboro Road
Morrow, Georgia 30260
Telephone: 770-968-2100
Fax: 770-968-2547
Email: atlanta.archives@nara.gov

**National Archives Southeast Region (Atlanta)**:
http://www.archives.gov/atlanta/finding-aids/index.html

**US Department of Veterans Affairs Nationwide Gravesite Locator** – includes information on veterans and their family members buried in veterans and military cemeteries having a government grave marker.

**US Department of Veterans Affairs Nationwide Gravesite Locator** link to: http://gravelocator.cem.va.gov/

You may also find your ancestor's military records in the following databases:

**United States General Index to Pension Files, 1861-1934**

**United States General Index to Pension Files, 1861-1934**: https://familysearch.org/search/collection/1919699

**United States Index to Service Records, War with Spain, 1898**

**United States Index to Service Records, War with Spain, 1898** link to: https://familysearch.org/search/collection/1919583

**United States Index to Indian Wars Pension Files, 1892-1926** – military pension records of soldiers who fought in the Indian Wars between 1817 and 1898

**United States Index to Indian Wars Pension Files, 1892-1926**: https://familysearch.org/search/collection/1979427

**United States Registers of Enlistments in the U.S. Army, 1798-1914** - index of men who enlisted in the United States Army, 1798-1914.

**United States Registers of Enlistments in the U.S. Army, 1798-1914** link to: https://familysearch.org/search/collection/1880762

**United States Mexican War Pension Index, 1887-1926** - index to Mexican War pension files for service between 1846 and 1848

**United States Mexican War Pension Index, 1887-1926**: https://familysearch.org/search/collection/1979390

**Civil War Soldiers Service Records** - Service records for both Union and Confederate soldiers indexed by soldier's name, rank, and unit.

**Civil War Soldier Service Records**:
http://go.fold3.com/civilwar_records/

North Carolina Cemetery Records

As convenient as it is to search cemetery records online, keep in mind that there are a few disadvantages over visiting a cemetery in person. They are:

- Tombstone information is not always accurately transcribed
- The arrangement of the graves in a cemetery can be crucial as family members are often buried next to each other or in the same grave. This arrangement is not always preserved in the alphabetical indexes that are found online.

With that information in mind, the following websites have databases that can be searched online for North Carolina Cemetery records.

**North Carolina Tombstone Transcription Project** - death and burial records

**North Carolina Tombstone Transcription Project** :
http://www.usgwtombstones.org/northcarolina/n-car.html

**African American Cemeteries Online** – African American, slave, and Native American cemetery records

**African American Cemeteries Online**:
http://africanamericancemeteries.com/ar/

**Access Genealogy** – database of North Carolina cemetery record transcriptions

**Access Genealogy**:
http://www.accessgenealogy.com/cemetery/north-carolina-cemetery-records.htm

**Find a Grave** – over 100 million grave records can be searched on this site. Search can be conducted by name, location, or cemetery name.

**Find a Grave** link to: http://www.findagrave.com/

**Interment.net** - A free online database containing approximately 4 million cemetery records from around the world.

**Interment.net**: http://www.interment.net/

**Billion Graves** – as the name implies, you can search a billion records including headstone photos, transcriptions, cemetery records, and grave locations.

**Billion Graves** :
http://billiongraves.com/pages/search/index.php#cemetery

North Carolina Obituaries

Obituaries can reveal a wealth about our ancestor and other relatives. You can search our **North Carolina Newspaper Obituaries Listings** from hundreds of North Carolina newspapers online for free.

**North Carolina Newspaper Obituaries Listings**:
http://obituarieshelp.org/north_carolina_newspaper_obituaries.html

North Carolina Wills and Probate Records

The documents found in a probate packet may include a complete inventory of a person's estate, newspaper entries, witness testimony, a copy of a will, list of debtors and creditors, names of executors or trustees, names of heirs. They can not only tell you about the ancestor you're currently researching, but lead to other ancestors.

**State Archives of North Carolina** – Wills and county court records dating from 18ᵗʰ century

State Archives of North Carolina
109 E. Jones St.
Raleigh, North Carolina 27601
Phone: (919) 733-3952

**State Archives of North Carolina**o:
http://www.ncdcr.gov/archives/Public/Collections.aspx

Family Search has the following online indexes which can be searched for free:

**North Carolina, County Records, 1833-1970**:
https://familysearch.org/search/collection/1916185

**North Carolina, Estate Files, 1663-1979**:
https://familysearch.org/search/collection/1911121

**North Carolina, Probate Records, 1735-1970**:
https://familysearch.org/search/collection/1867501

**North Carolina, State Supreme Court Case Files, 1800-1909**:
https://familysearch.org/search/collection/1878751

## North Carolina Immigration and Naturalization Records

The naturalization process generated many types of records, including petitions, declarations of intention, and oaths of allegiance. These records can provide family historians with information such as a person's birth date and place of birth, immigration year, marital status, spouse information, occupation, witnesses' names and addresses, and more.

**State Archives of North Carolina** – Naturalization certificates and petitions from early 18th century

State Archives of North Carolina
109 E. Jones St.
Raleigh, North Carolina 27601
Phone: (919) 733-3952

**State Archives of North Carolina**:
http://www.ncdcr.gov/archives/Public/Collections.aspx

**National Archives Southeast Region (Atlanta)** – Records of Admission to Citizenship, U.S. District Court, Charleston, SC.,1790-1906, Naturalization Records, and Passenger Lists from all US East Coast Ports dating from 1820

5780 Jonesboro Road
Morrow, Georgia 30260
Telephone: 770-968-2100
Fax: 770-968-2547
Email: atlanta.archives@nara.gov

**National Archives Southeast Region (Atlanta)**:
http://www.archives.gov/atlanta/finding-aids/index.html

Family Search has the following online index which can be searched for free:

**North Carolina, Wilmington and Morehead City Passenger and Crew Lists, 1908-1958**:
https://familysearch.org/search/collection/2072744

North Carolina Native American Records

**National Archives Southeast Region (Atlanta)** – Native American census schedules, Native American Freedman's lists, records of the Bureau of Indian Affairs, Dawes Commission Enrollment cards, Emigration Rolls, Annuity Rolls, and more

5780 Jonesboro Road
Morrow, Georgia 30260
Telephone: 770-968-2100
Fax: 770-968-2547
Email: atlanta.archives@nara.gov

**National Archives Southeast Region (Atlanta)**:
http://www.archives.gov/atlanta/finding-aids/index.html

**Access Genealogy** – North Carolina Native American census records, tribal histories, and much more

**Access Genealogy**: http://www.accessgenealogy.com/native/north-carolina-indian-tribes.htm

**U.S. National Archives** - information on American Indians who maintained their ties to Federally-recognized Tribes (1830-1970).

**U.S. National Archives**: http://www.archives.gov/research/native-americans/

**Records of the Bureau of Indian Affairs (BIA)**

**Records of the Bureau of Indian Affairs (BIA)** link to:
http://www.archives.gov/research/guide-fed-records/groups/075.html

**American Indians Records Repository** - records dating from the 1700s including trust, education and other historic Indian Affairs records

American Indian Records Repository
Meritex Enterprises
17501 West 98th Street
Lenexa, KS 66219
Phone: 913-888-0601

**American Indians Records Repository**:
http://www.doi.gov/ost/records_mgmt/american-indian-records-repository.cfm

## Missing Matriarchs – Resources for Researching Female North Carolina Ancestors

Looking for female ancestors requires an adjustment of how we view traditional records sources. A woman's identity was often under that of her husband, and often individual records for them can be difficult to locate. The following resources are effective in locating female ancestors in North Carolina where traditional records may not reveal them.

### Bibliographies

1. *North Carolina Quilts,* Ruth Robeson (University of North Carolina Press, 1988)
2. *North Carolina Women of the Confederacy,* Lucy L. Anderson (The United Daughters of the Confederacy, 1926)
3. *By Her Own Bootstraps: A Saga of Women in North Carolina,* Albert Coates (The Author, 1975)
4. *Women of Guilford County North Carolina: A Study of Women's Contributions, 1740-1979,* Paula S. Jordan (Women of Guilford, 1979)

### Selected Resources for North Carolina Women's History

Afro-American Women's Collection
Thomas F. Holgate Library
900 East Washington St.
Greensboro, NC 27420

Triangle Multicultural Women's History Project
605 Germaine St.
Apex, NC 27502

Women's Studies Reference Archivist
William R. Perkins Library
Duke University
Box 90185
Durham, NC 27708-0185

## Common North Carolina Surnames

The following surnames are among the most common in North Carolina and are also being currently researched by other genealogists. If you find your surname here, there is a chance that some research has already been performed on your ancestor.

Acord, Albertson, Allen, Austin, Barringer, Bass, Beatenbo, Belangia, Belcher, Billings, Black, Blackwelder, Blackwell, Bolton, Bradford, Britt, Brown, Bryan, Busby, Carlton, Carrothers, Carruthers, Carter, Cauble, Cecil, Channel, Childress, Christy, Clay, Cook, Cooke, Corker, Crowley, Davies, Deanie, Dorton, Douglas, Draper, Driggers, Duncan, Elizabeth, Epperson, Erwin, Eudy, Fink, Fisher, Ford, Forrest, Fortner, Foster, Frances, Freeman, French, Garmon, Goodman, Grant, Green, Griffin, Harden, Hare, Harkey, Hasting, Haywood, Heintz, Helms, Henshaw, Herche, Hill, Hinson, Holleman, Hopkins, Howell, Hudson, Hughes, Jones, Joyner, Kelow, Kerr, Kindley, Kiser, Kluttz, Knowles, Knox, Lamb, Locklear, Long, Lungstrum, Mary, Mc Crauy, McDaniel, Meggs, Miller, Milly, Mitchell, Moose, Motley, Mullis, Mumford, Mumms, Munford, Muth, Myers, Nance, Nichols, Pace, Parmely, Pate, Pearis, Peters, Petrea, Pfaul, Polson, Pressley, Riggs, Robinson, Robison, Roddy, Rosanah, Rowell, Royall, Rucker, Rusk, Ruth, Safrit, Scott, Seamone, Sehorn, Sellers, Shelby, Shrewsbury, Sizemore, Smith, Snyder, Speer, Spradling, Stamper, Starnes, Steen, Stegall, Stephens, Stewart, Stuart, Sutton, Teator, Thompson, Townsend, Turner, Turpin, Tyler, Walker, Walraven, Walton, Washington, Watkins, Watter, Weigand, Whiteker, Williamson, Wilson, Windham, Woman, Woolridge, Wright, Young, Yount

## About the Author

Gary L. Morris worked from 2009 to 2014 as a professional researcher for a major player in the genealogy field. After tracing his family lineage back to 1683, he has decided to publish these helpful guides to share the valuable information he has discovered during his career to help others trace their family lineages. An avid genealogist himself, he hopes you will find this guide factual, thorough, helpful, and most of all, effective in helping you to find your family members.